CHRISTCHURCH
— The Golden Years —

MICHAEL A. HODGES

DORSET BOOKS

First published in Great Britain in 2003
Reprinted 2006
Copyright © 2003 Michael A. Hodges

British Library Cataloguing-in-Publication Data
A CIP record for this title is available from the British Library

ISBN 1 871164 38 9
ISBN 978 1 871164 38 1

For Joan

DORSET BOOKS
Official Publisher to Dorset County Council

Halsgrove House
Lower Moor Way
Tiverton EX16 6SS
T: 01884 243242
F: 01884 243325

sales@halsgrove.com
www.halsgrove.com

Printed and bound in Great Britain
by CPI, Bath

CONTENTS

ACKNOWLEDGEMENTS

The majority of photographs used in this book were taken by Allen White, 1919–97. He was born in Boscombe, the younger of two brothers, the eldest of whom became a vicar. Allen White first worked for Fairey Aviation at Hamble, and during the Second World War joined the RAF and worked as a photographer in the Middle East and Europe. After the war he set up his own photographic business in Christchurch and also worked with the *Christchurch Times*. He later became the staff photographer at the Military Engineering Experimental Establishment at Christchurch Barracks where he met his wife. They had two daughters but later divorced. Allen was a founder member of the Christchurch Local History Society and produced some eleven publications on local history and areas of the town. He was later made an Honorary Life Member and was further honoured by the Society creating the Allen White Award for members' work. The Borough Council in 1992 granted him the Borough's Meritorious Service Award for his contribution to the community through his work and publications.

The book could also not have been prepared without the active assistance of the staff of the Red House Museum at Christchurch and particularly the co-operation provided by John Lewis, a senior museum assistant who is also a well-known photographer. The museum is interesting in that although being situated in Dorset it is administered by the Hampshire County Council Museum Service, the two counties and Christchurch borough each bearing a third of the cost.

The Christchurch Local History Society also co-operated by providing access to their photographic library in the Local History Room of Dorset County Council's Druitt Library, in the town's High Street.

Where individual photographers are known they are identified by name; in the case of Allen White only initials are used.

However, many photographs are anonymous since the source library does not have the information.

Allen White with his aerial photograph camera in the co-pilot seat of a doorless light aircraft at Christchurch (Somerford) Airfield.

INTRODUCTION

Christchurch is an historic town at the confluence of the Avon and Stour, with its origins in the prehistory of Christchurch Harbour. It has seen Roman, Saxon and Norman invasions, and has been defended against the threat of Viking, French and German invaders; all of these defences have left their remains. This photographic record deals with the latter half of the twentieth century, a time of peace. Yet it was also a time of great development for the borough, when the growth in population and building has been more rapid than at any other time in its history.

A book of photographs can rarely be a complete or balanced history of a period since it depends on the accidents of photographic action and then the coincidence of subsequent availability of photographs to an author. I am, therefore, grateful to all of those who have supplied illustrations, especially to the Christchurch Local History Society and most particularly the Red House Museum.

Christchurch once included Bournemouth which has now far outgrown its parent. The coast of South East Dorset is one urban area from Upton, through Poole, Bournemouth and Christchurch to the boundary with the New Forest at Highcliffe. Poole and Bournemouth are both unitary authorities; Christchurch borough is part of Dorset County. Until 1974 both Bournemouth and Christchurch were part of Hampshire. In *Domesday*, Christchurch was one of only three boroughs in all of Hampshire. Christchurch is the smallest urban authority which survived the 1974 reorganisation.

Economically, Christchurch once depended on water transport, for both the west trade and for smuggling. The latter was once the main industry of the inhabitants. The arrival of the railway in the mid-nineteenth century enabled a tourist trade to develop and gave opportunities to commute to work further afield. The beautiful harbour, rivers and coast, with its proximity of the New Forest made the area very popular as a retirement location as well as for visitors. Christchurch is full of history and heritage which is one of its main attractions for tourists.

Photographic Code

CLHS
Christchurch Local History Society (many photographs may be by Allen White but have not been so recorded).

RHM
Red House Museum (some photographs may also be by Allen White but not so recorded).

AW
Allen White, photographer.

Where photographs are by a known photographer in either CLHS or RHM collections the name is given. The author and publisher have done their joint and several best to ascribe and describe the pictures correctly; should any unforseen error or ommission have occurred they would welcome communication from readers.

CLHS

This picture of the Priory Church shows, from left to right: Lady Chapel with St Michael's Loft (one-time Grammar School) above; north transept above one of the crypts (which may contain Saxon work); north aisle and nave (started in Norman times); north porch (once used for town meetings); tower (built by Edward IV). The parapet on the left above St Michael's Loft stops short where work ceased at the Dissolution of the Monasteries in 1539. The Norman Dean of Christchurch, Ranulf Flambard started the nave in 1094. At the time the town was called Tweoxneam, (the place) 'betwixt the waters'. Ranulf of the Waters was named by Gerald of Wales as the man who shot King William Rufus dead in the New Forest, rather than Walter Tryell the man more usually blamed by history, though this has never been established.

❧

PRIORY

Christchurch Castle and Priory from the north. On the left is the Mill Stream next to the Constable's Hall, with the bowling green in the bailey between the hall and the keep on the motte.

Christchurch High Street, Priory and Harbour from the north, c.1950. Top left is Hengistbury Head; bottom left the allotments cover the Saxon wall, discovered in 1970, of the burgh of Tweoxneam. Bottom right is the road junction of High Street with Bargates and Barrack Road, before the bypass split the town in two.

Town Quay, the Priory and Elkin's Boat Yard on Convent Meadows. The Bandstand, given to the town in 1938, is visible centre left. Also visible is Place Mill and the old sailing club building, which concealed a Home Guard machine-gun post.

The footpath through the churchyard to the north porch of the Priory was once lined by an avenue of elm trees, which became casualties of Dutch Elm disease in the 1950s.

RHM AW

Priory House was built in the monastic precinct in 1777, by Gustav Brander who wrote the first book on British fossils, at Barton-on-Sea (once part of Christchurch Hundred). It was here that Prince Louis Phillipe, future King of France, once stayed during the Napoleonic Wars. The Priory House is built only a fathom from the south side of the church.

CLHS R. Adams

Revd Basil Trevor-Morgan, vicar of the Priory in 1979, receives a cheque from the Mayor's Charity for its maintenance. Every Christchurch mayor nominates a charity or charities at the start of their year in office.

RHM AW

The Priory roof from the Priory Tower, showing the Avon beyond. Three stair towers are visible beyond the transepts. In a great storm of 1703 lead on the roof was rolled up like carpet. The roof of St Michael's Loft above the Lady Chapel at the east end is at a slight angle from the rest of the roof.

CLHS M. Tizzard

Close Helmet of 1540 found in a Priory cupboard in the 1950s (when the author was a youth) and taken by him in the 1970s to the Tower Armouries for attention. The helmet is attached to a 1640s pikeman's gorget and was probably part of a funerary monument. It may have been in use against the French invasion of the Isle of Wight in 1544, while the gorget may have been used in the siege of Christchurch Castle in 1645. The helmet is now in the St Michael's Loft Museum at the Priory.

CLHS

Priory, Castle, High Street, Castle Street and Town Bridge. The area between the Priory, churchyard, Castle and Mill Stream was known as 'The Werkes' and was where stone was landed for building the Priory and the Castle. The area is now known as 'Paradise'. The tree-covered area at the top left is Druitt Gardens.

CHURCH STREET

Gateway to Priory churchyard with Church Hatch and the Castle keep beyond. The keep has walls over 8ft thick and was slighted after the Civil War, during which it withstood a three-day close siege. As a result the Governor, a major, was promoted to Lt-Col and made Governor of Winchester.

Cottage in Church Street in 1971. Ye Olde Eight Bells on the right was a pub until 1907. It was named because the Priory peal was once seven bells (it is now 12), so the pub was like the 19th Hole for golfers, where the bell-ringers enjoyed the 'eighth bell'! It was a well-known smugglers' pub where on one occasion a women foiled a Revenue search by sitting on a tub of brandy under her skirts while she attended to a baby. Note that the roofs still have some stone shingles, thatch being a fire risk.

Church Street and Castle Street, originally straight in the Saxon town, have been forced into curves by the erection of the Norman motte of the Castle. However, the access from Wick Lane has not been affected; it was once an extension of Castle Street. Church Lane is also unaffected although it once may have continued across Church Street to where the Castle now stands. The houses on the east side of Church Street and the south side of Castle Street are built over the Castle ditch.

The centre of this picture shows the trolleybus turntable – which has survived redevelopments and may now be the only one remaining in the country – with a trolleybus upon it. The road junction of Church Street, Castle Street and High Street forms what was once the Market Square, in which stood the Market Hall, now the Mayor's Parlour; this was removed over 150 years ago to the High Street. The Palladian mansion on the west side of the Square was Square House which unfortunately was demolished in 1958.

CLHS

The bottom centre of this picture shows the Red House Museum and its gardens. This building in Quay Road was once the borough's Workhouse. Bottom right is Church Hatch, and top right the King's Arms Hotel. Square House is at the top centre of the picture, so it was taken before 1958, with a trolleybus on the turntable. St Margaret's Avenue is at bottom left, with Whitehall–Church Lane running left to right at the bottom third of the picture, and Wick Lane at the top third.

RHM AW

A trolleybus being manoeuvred on the turntable, with the conductor adjusting the boom and the driver providing the motive power. The Dolphin Inn on the right was a casualty of redevelopment in 1973 but the turntable survives.

RHM AW

Church Street is seen in 1988 showing the Dolphin site after redevelopment, a sympathetic design which is in keeping with the town. However, some such new ventures have experienced problems in letting owing to rents and business rates.

No. 4 Church Lane, a typical town-centre cottage, undergoes rethatching. At one time the harbour reed beds were in demand for thatch, which would last for many years.

The junction of Castle Street and Church Street with the Castle keep beyond, seen in 1973. The Black Bull Inn was once in this area.

HIGH STREET

CLHS

Square House, High Street, a mansion built in 1776, was demolished in 1958 despite boasting Adam ceilings and fireplaces. The building was owned by John Cook, a wealthy brewer whose premises were behind Square House. He owned a sloop, the Stour, *which was used in smuggling – and was Mayor five times! In those days everyone was involved in 'The Trade'.*

CLHS

Square House in the mid 1950s with the annual Church Parade of the St John's Ambulance Brigade Cadets.

RHM

Back garden of Square House c.1954, now the site of the town's main post office (earmarked as a potential site for redevelopment).

*An arcade, which leads to the post office, with Fine Fair to the left and Courts to the right, replaced Square House.
The council planners approved this horror in place of the eighteenth-century Palladian mansion which formerly
stood here. What price progress!*

Ye Olde George Inn, originally the St George and Dragon Inn, once a coach stop for the Emerald on the Lymington to Poole run. It was known as a haunt for smugglers and like so many old buildings in the town has a reputation for ghosts.

The site of the old Market Square from the coach exit from Ye Olde George Inn. The Market Hall, now the Mayor's Parlour, stood in this square from 1745 to 1859.

Clingan's House, which takes its name from a former owner who founded a charity in 1736 for young people to enter a trade, is shown c.1960 when occupied by Smith's furniture shop. The charity still operates.

James Bochan, landlord of the Fisherman's Haunt, leading Santa Claus and the Snow Queen Christmas Parade. James, born in the Ukraine, stayed in Britain after the Second World War, created a successful business and became a much loved local character.

View from the then United Reformed Church Tower at Millhams Lane, showing the rear of east side and front of west side of High Street, looking south. Hengtisbury Head is visible beyond the Priory.

The Ship Inn, which holds the oldest licence in Christchurch. Like many other old pubs in the borough it was once much frequented by smugglers.

The junction of Millhams Lane, once also known as Meeting House Lane, with the High Street. This was probably once a Saxon cross-roads linking Druitt Gardens to the Mill Stream. On the left is the tower of the Nonconformist church which has at various times been Congregational, United Reformed and is now Elim. The Nonconformists took over the Priory after the Civil War but were ejected on the Restoration in 1660. They then met secretly in private houses and on St Catherine's Hill until they built their church in 1816, which was replaced by the present building in 1867. The building on the right was known as the Old Tolsey, since it was the toll-house for the market, still held in the High Street on Mondays. A link between the roof of the Old Tolsey and the adjacent Ship Inn was probably built to accommodate the transfer of smuggled goods between the two buildings.

Staggs, the last of the many mercers of Christchurch, in about 1955. Such operators of the wool trade had a long local history. Christchurch merchants helped finance the Poole–Newfoundland trade.

The east side of the High Street, looking north, with Staggs, Baxter's and the Market Hall (now Mayor's Parlour) – and a trolleybus.

Shop fronts change but the façade and roof line above can remain unchanged, thus retaining some atmosphere of heritage. On the left is visible part of the former Civic Offices which were accommodated in what was once a technical school until the present offices were built in Bridge Street.

The Hengist Masonic Lodge, now a solicitor's office.

The Mayor's Parlour when the ground floor was still in use as offices. It has since been restored to be an open area for stalls, as when it was first a Market Hall in 1745.

The Mayor's Parlour illuminated for Christmas 1978. The Christchurch mayors operate a Christmas Goodwill Fund every year which raises money to seek to help the lonely or poor at Christmas. The past mayors assist the current incumbent of the post in determining allocations.

Christchurch Monday Market, which existed from as early as 1149, was closed for about 100 years from 1872. Fortunately, it was resumed and this picture shows the market c.1978 in what later became Saxon Square.

The opening of Saxon Square, 28 September 1983. In the background is the Mayor's Parlour with the offices removed from beneath. Halls of this type would have begun as a roof over a meeting place such as a market cross. Later fire brooms and other equipment were hung under the roof. Later still the Hall would be rebuilt as a first-floor room on stilts, like the present building, for the market to shelter beneath and the burgesses to have their meetings above. Under the stairs an enclosed space could be used as a lock-up. In the foreground is a modern stone cross designed to represent Celtic-Saxon carvings.

Allen White standing in the fireplace of Hookey's House. This medieval building stood on the east side of the High Street, north of the Mayor's Parlour.

CLHS

Hookey's House. Samuel Hookey was a successful smuggler, and mayor, who owned three luggers. He started life as a blacksmith's apprentice in Pound Lane in the eighteenth century. His house is of fourteenth-century origin, as shown by the cruck construction.

RHM

The roof of Hookey's House reveals that ships' timbers were reused in making the roof, and also that the building was once thatched.

25

A model to show how Hookey's House was constructed, with the original medieval frame being added to by a raised roof and additional skin. The south end had been extended and contained stone Tudor-style, mullion windows.

The former Midland Bank, a building of some dignity, which gave its name to Bank Close. It is now HSBC.

Keith Motors' garage used to stand in the High Street between the Midland Bank and Bow House. It was about here that the Bargate once stood in the street.

The Fountain Hotel at the junction of High Street with Sopers Lane and Barrack Road. The name Fountain derives from the drinking trough which once stood in the street at this point. A well in the area next to the building once had a smugglers' hide cut into its wall.

CASTLE STREET

Constable's Hall seen from Quartley's Bridge in Castle Street. This was once the luxurious residence of the Constable of Christchurch Castle and the centre of local administration. The building dates from about 1150 and is now owned by English Heritage. It has been suggested that it would benefit from having its roof restored, as has been done with a similar building at Ludlow in Shropshire.

Mill Stream and north side of Quartley's Bridge, with Constable's Hall visible beyond. This stream was once a military defence for the Saxon burgh as well as the water supply for the town's mills. Near where this photograph was taken was once the site of the ducking stool when the stream was at least six feet deep.

King's Arms Hotel, in a prominent position opposite the Castle and the bowling green. This hotel was once used to accommodate the South Hants Militia in 1794 before Christchurch Barracks was complete. In the nineteenth century it was called Humby's Commercial Hotel after its then owner.

RHM AW

New Forest Perfumery and Tea Shop, 11 Castle Street, once a butcher's shop. It is Christchurch borough's oldest council house, and is often wrongly called the Old Court House. The latter stood to the left of the picture in what is now an empty space in which the old town stocks have been placed.

Lloyds Bank with Drum Alley between it and the Olde George Inn. The 'Drum' leads from what was the Square to Ducking Stool Lane. The brick skin of the bank building surrounds three older structures which may, like Hookey's House, contain medieval elements.

MILLHAMS STREET

Castle Street is seen running east–west from bottom to top of the photograph. High Street runs across the top and Millhams Street runs north–south across to centre of the picture. The trees at the bottom line the banks of the Mill Stream.

Ducking Stool Lane from the junction of Drum Alley with Millhams Street. The lane runs down to the Mill Stream and the site of the Ducking Pool. The Ducking Stool, like the Whirly Gigg, was kept in the north porch of the Priory and taken down Church Street and Drum Alley to Ducking Stool Lane when required.

RHM AW

Some inhabitants of Millhams Street on Coronation Day, 1953.

RHM AW

Demolition of cottages taking place in Millhams Street in 1971. Regrettably, opportunities for archaeological investigation within the Saxon burgh, were not taken up before the 1970s.

RHM AW

Nos 5 to 8 Millhams Street east side before demolition for redevelopment.

Cottages on the west side of Millhams Street.

CLHS

Millhams Meade House, on the northeast side of Millhams Street, in 1991.

Looking east down Millhams Lane to Millhams Meade in Millhams Street. The building on the right displaying details of the Ship Inn car park was one of the town's former fusee chain factories, demolished in 1965. These establishments employed women, girls and paupers from the Workhouse, putting them at grave risk of eye strain.

WICK-WHITEHALL

The Red House Museum garden. Once the Workhouse, the museum opened in 1951 and in 1974 was taken over by Hampshire County Council who operate an excellent museum service.

Restoration work in the roof space of Place Mill area in 1970. The original mill is mentioned in Domesday. *The word 'place' harks back to the original name of Tweoxneam, meaning the place between the waters.*

The bridge over the Mill Stream at Place Mill, linking the Quay area to Convent Meadows. The arches of this bridge are possibly of Saxon origin.

Mrs Toms in her cottage at Church Lane, a road which at the Silver Street junction becomes Whitehall, c.1971. The Saxon burgh wall originally ran to this area, after which the River Stour was the main defence.

RHM AW

The photograph shows the oldest part of the town, looking southwest: the island formed by the Avon on the left, Clay Pool at the top right, and Wick Lane running from centre right to the High Street, with Whitehall running parallel above it, linked to it by Silver Street.

No. 3 Whitehall in 1971, a thatched cottage now surrounded by housing.

The Fountain in a new location at Quomps, having been moved from the north end of the High Street. It is now relocated at Bargates. The cottages were demolished in the 1970s for new development.

The aftermath of a helicopter disaster in 1969 at Christchurch Regatta, when two in a formation of four hit rotor blades and crashed, fortunately missing the crowds. But the pilot of this machine was killed after it hit the roof of a Whitehall cottage and exploded in the back garden.

The other machine crashed in Wick Lane. Here members of the Army Air Corps are removing the wreckage.

Cottages in Wick Lane.

St Margaret's Avenue in 1950. Over the succeeding twenty years the area was fully developed.

The Hayloft, Wick Lane, at the junction with Silver Street, c.1989. The building is now used by the Christchurch and District Arts Council.

THE STOUR

The right centre of the photograph shows Town Quay and Clay Pool where the Avon enters the Stour. Beyond lies Christchurch Harbour, with Stanpit Marsh centre left, Mudeford Spit in the background and the Isle of Wight on the horizon.

Christchurch Town Quay in 1970, photographed from the top of Place Mill, looking up the Stour.

RHM AW

Skating on Clay Pool, off Town Quay, in the harsh winter of 1963.

CLHS

The local swans look puzzled by the ice at Town Quay in 1963.

RHM

Skaters head happily for the frozen harbour, 1963.

RHM AW

Here the impromptu ice rink is the River Stour at Quomps, 1963.

CLHS

A very different scene as floods engulf Quomps in 1979. The town centre has since been protected by flood barriers. At the time the Jumpers area at Iford off the Stour suffered most.

The Avon meanders through Millhams water-meadows in the background. The United Reformed Church, Regent Cinema and former pumping station are the three prominent building seen from top to bottom of the photograph. In the foreground is the Stour with the Regatta fair at Quomps.

This photograph taken in 1947 shows the site which became first the Wick Ferry Holiday Camp, then Pontin's Holiday Camp and now housing (with a hoped-for hotel). A Second World War motor torpedo boat lies on the Bournemouth bank of the Stour.

A sea-fishing boat on the Stour, off Wick Ferry Holiday Camp; note the MTB beyond, now a houseboat.

The River Stour at the site which became the Quomps slipway and Rowing Club landing.

Wick Ferry Holiday Camp on the River Stour.

Riverside at Wick Ferry Holiday Camp, c.1960.

Reception of Wick Ferry Holiday Camp.

The newly opened Pontin's Holiday Camp and Quomps car park from above.

A school outing at Wick Ferry landing.

This car was pulled from the Stour two days after it had been driven in error down the slipway next to Pontin's on the opposite bank. The car was invisible and only traced by a trail of oil spotted after the two ladies who had been in the car were missed.

A pontoon on the east bank of Stour, south of Tuckton Bridge. Some years after this picture was taken, a child was drowned near here when an unstable pontoon turned over on him. The site has now been developed for housing.

Tuckton Bridge over the Stour in 1960 pictured before development between Stour Road and Soper's Lane along the Stour. On the right, south of the bridge, is an island which contains a large pill-box for a heavy weapon; part of the Christchurch Anti-Tank Island defence 1940–44.

Tuckton Bridge Toll House on the northeast side of the bridge. (The author's wife recalls that it was one penny for an adult and a halfpence for a pram, when her mother took her over).

Roadworks at Tuckton Bridge, a favourite pastime of utility companies in Christchurch.

Tucktonia, a large selection of miniature model buildings which lasted for around ten years from the mid-1970s. The site is now occupied by a private marina, houses and flats. Like Quomps the area is made up of land infilled with assorted materials.

✦
BRIDGE STREET

Waterloo Bridge and part of Bridge Street before 1978.

RHM AW

CLHS

Town Bridge and part of Waterloo Bridge, illustrating the different style of arches used, the latter being the more modern of the two, dating from the early-nineteenth century. Boats of 25 tons burden used to travel up the Avon to Salisbury until 1735. The island south of Bridge Street is now much developed, its smart town houses having been built with boat owners in mind.

Here the flood waters have affected Stoney Lane, where such problems can still occur. This is probably as a result of over-development on water-meadows (which were designed to flood) and the canalisation of rivers, along with increased rapid rainfall run-off from roofs and roads.

Magnolia House, Stony Lane, c.1970.

Purewell in 1955. Interestingly, the factory roofs still have wartime camouflage.

BARGATES AND BYPASS

Looking south down Bargates from Fairmile Bridge over the railway. The trolleybus on the right is turning into Stour Road.

High Street, showing junction with Bargates at bottom right. With no bypass yet, it is probably about 1955.

RHM AW

The Mill Stream runs diagonally from bottom left to lower right, with High Street and Bargates running parallel and, as there is no bypass, the date must be about 1950. The Saxon wall of the town was discovered twenty years later, under the allotment-type gardens in the left centre, running from the Mill Stream, under the line of the path through the allotments, across High Street, then under Bank Close, until it meets Druitt Gardens, where it turns sharp left.

The Antelope Hotel in the centre of the picture stands on a large traffic island facing the High Street. The Cross Keys Inn was once in this area. The island is bounded by: Bargates, Barrack Road and the now-lost Spicer Street. A trolleybus is entering Bargates near the Assembly Rooms (Conservative Club). There is as yet still no bypass to split the town in two.

The Brewery Tower, which used to stand west of some yards behind Bow House. It was demolished in the late 1950s. At one time Christchurch had three breweries, and until piped water was laid on it was safer to drink 'small beer' (weak beer) than the local well water. This was a result of the length of time people had lived in one place on porous gravel cut by wells, cess and rubbish pits.

RHM AW

CLHS

The entrance to the High Street in 1945. The drinking fountain and water trough is shown in its original location on the right of the photograph, and gave its name to the Fountain Hotel. Brewery House projects into High Street to cause a narrowing as in the days of the Bargate, which was removed in the first half of the eighteenth century. The Green Tree Inn once stood on the left in the High Street.

The Antelope Hotel was an impressive building that became one of the many casualties of the coming of the bypass. On the right a no-entry sign marks the access from Pound Lane.

The Pound, a pen for stray animals, was controlled by the hayward who was also the town crier. The job of hayward was an appointment of the Court Leet who also elected the bailiff, two constables, ten tythingmen, scavenger, inspector of chimneys, aletaster and breadweigher.

CHRISTCHURCH – THE GOLDEN YEARS

The restaurant named 1654AD in Bargates on the site of the Horse and Groom, its deed being dated from 1654, during the time of The Commonwealth. The site is now a Chinese restaurant. In 1977 the owner of the restaurant permitted the author to use Manpower Service Commission labour to dig a 2 x 70 metre trench in the back garden. This revealed Saxon grave goods and so a major excavation was carried out. As a result two Bronze Age barrows were found and a Saxon pagan cemetery of the sixth century. This confirmed the early-Saxon origins of Christchurch, contemporary with the high-status pagan cemetery further up the Avon at Breamore.

The Georgian House, Bargates, once an antique shop, before demolition for the bypass. There is a real market opportunity for antique shops in Christchurch.

The building of the bypass in 1957, gave rise to most of the planning, economic and traffic problems now faced by Christchurch town centre. Planned by Hampshire County Council, it cut the town in two while introducing volumes of traffic seeking to get to places beyond. A Christchurch Relief Road is much needed but does not feature in Dorset County Council plans at present.

Barrack Road and the junction with Spicer Street before the development of the Fountain Roundabout.

The opening of the bypass with Christchurch's Mayor, Cllr John Richardson, in attendance.

Barrack Road and the Pit Site Fire Station. Nowadays a purpose-built fire station exists at Fairmile. The Pit Site, once a gravel pit, also at one time held the town jail, called the 'blind house' since the original lock-up, under the Market Hall stairs, had no windows. Stocks also stood on the site.

Another view of Barrack Road before the police station was built, c.1965. The Duke of Wellington Inn on the right, one of several pubs which grew out of the arrival of the barracks after 1794, survived the development.

The bypass is nearly completed in this picture but no start has been yet made on the Fountain Roundabout.

The new Fountain Roundabout viewed from above Pound Lane. The new police station stands centre right, behind the old fusee chain factory. The Barrack Road Recreation Ground opposite the police station is all that remains of the Portfield.

The fusee chain factory and Hart's House, Bargates c.1950. Fusee chains were used in clocks and watches throughout the eighteenth and nineteenth centuries. Some 500 people were employed in three local factories at Bridge Street, Millhams Lane and Bargates, plus outwork in cottages. Most of the work was done by women and girls, often paupers from the Workhouse. The delicate eye-straining work often caused problems and recourse was made to the curative properties of Purewell and Tutton's Well, as in medieval times.

Euonymous, a cottage at Bargates which was demolished 1971.

NORTH OF THE TOWN

Knapp Mill c.1960. The Domesday Book *refers to a mill at Knapp. It is now a base of the local water company.*

It took much effort to shift this mature tree at the junction of Fairmile and The Grove, c.1960, but now would probably be protected by a Tree Preservation Order.

Jumpers House in 1934, bombed during the Second World War and subsequently demolished. The name Jumpers derived from Juniper. Jumpers is now a local place-name.

The garden of the Red House Museum, probably in 1951 when the museum first opened. On the left is John Lavender, the original curator, with next to him the vicar, Canon Price. The Mayoress is in the centre, on the right of the Mayor, Cllr Ken Smith. The others are probably members of the museum's first committee, while it was still a private institution.

Druitt House, now Druitt Library at 15 High Street, was named after the family who lived there. Herbert Druitt had his own collection of antiquities in the Red House which he had owned and which gave rise to the museum there. Before the museum officially opened in 1951 there was much sorting out to be done. Here, acting curator R.D. Moore is seen sorting books – and sundry other items – at Druitt House.

The Mayor, Cllr John Morgan, an ex-RAF man, at the west entrance of the Priory with Royal Air Force Association standards after a Battle of Britain Memorial Service.

RHM

CLHS G. Armit

Mayor, Cllr James Beattie, and Mayoress, Mrs E. Beattie, bearing their badges of office, about to set off for a Buckingham Palace garden party. Mayors only wear their chain of office inside their own borough, otherwise badges alone are worn. The Beatties are accompanied by Cllr and Mrs Hodges. Both men had served in the Royal Engineers and as officers of Customs and Excise.

CLHS

A past mayors' dinner is held, at private expense, every year, on this occasion at the Fisherman's Haunt. Those in the photograph are, back row (all past mayors): Fox, Beauchamp, Myers, Smith, Spreadbury, Hodges, Bruce, Morgan, Mrs Fox (Christchurch is unique in having a married couple who have both been mayors); centre row (all past mayoresses): Mesdames Kidman, Beauchamp, Myers, Bentley, Spreadbury, Hodges, Bruce, Winfield, Moss, ? ; front row (all past mayors): Kidman, Moss, Bentley, Winfield.

CLHS D. Penman

In 1992 Allen White was honoured for his historical and photographic work with the Borough's Meritorious Award. In this photograph Allen is receiving the Award from the Mayor and Mayoress, Cllr and Mrs Colin Bungy.

THE BARRACKS

Barrack Road was widened c.1960 at the expense of some of the Recreation Ground, the former Portfield, i.e. the field belonging to the town (port) with a market. The 'Rec' is all that is left after enclosures of what was once the town's common field. The photograph is looking towards the one-time site of the St Mary Magdalen Hospital for Lepers. The charity still exists, now combined with others.

Looking towards the Recreation Ground from the Barrack Road Bridge over the railway. The White Hart Hotel on the left was demolished in the 1980s for flats which have retained the name. The pub was no doubt at one time frequented by troops from Christchurch Barracks.

Christchurch Barracks, 1794–1994, from the air c.1948 when it was the Military Engineering Experimental Establishment (MEXE). The Bailey Bridge had been invented here early in the war. The original barracks for half a troop of cavalry was contained within the rectangle with long sides running from Barrack Road on the left. The guardroom is on the left, the Officers' Mess at the bottom right. The original barrack block was above the stables and is the long building with many dormers in the roof towards the right of the picture. Concrete anti-tank blocks are still along the north (barracks) side of the railway, part of the Christchurch Anti-Tank Island.

A more developed MEXE, which had several names varying from Experimental Bridging Establishment to Military Vehicle Experimental Establishment. This photograph shows that much of the original barracks' rectangular shape has been lost.

The guardroom, built 1811, remains. The picture dates from about 1970. This is where during the Second World War one sentry accidentally shot another.

The original stable block with barracks above, built 1794. It is reputedly haunted by a soldier of the First World War.

The Officers' Mess, now converted to flats.

Drawing Office staff in the frame at MEXE c.1970.

A pontoon bailey across the Stour at MEXE tests the weight of a tank transporter and main battle tank.

A parade of equipment leaving the barracks, possibly to take part in the Freedom Parade.

Freedom of the Borough Parade, 6 May 1969. The Freedom was granted to MEXE, it has also been granted to the Royal Hampshires, now merged with the Princess of Wales Royal Regiment, also to the Devon and Dorset Regiment. The Royal Engineers parade with the freedom scroll, band playing, swords drawn, bayonets fixed.

These beaches at Highcliffe had been protected with mines which had to be taken up again, often creating problems. Two Sappers were killed lifting mines at Avon Run Road in 1944. The barbed wire in this photograph may be a remnant of such minefield warnings.

Part of Christchurch Anti-Tank Island defence, a heavy-weapon pillbox on an island at Tuckton, to cover the bridge. Photographed in 1970s, it is still there, much overgrown.

An outwork of the Anti-Tank Island located within Christchurch MEXE at the barracks, to cover the northwest approach to the town.

A brick pillbox at Knapp near the waterworks. This box was part of a hedgehog defence in front of the Anti-Tank Island. It was to be manned by No. 17 Platoon of E Company 7th Battalion of Hampshire Regiment Home Guard. This Company of the Boscombe Battalion was responsible for the defence of Christchurch. The box has been removed and the site is covered by houses.

These concrete cubes are anti-tank obstacles in the old Railway Goods Yard at Fairmile. They are scheduled as Dorset Ancient Monument 832 and were for some years Britain's most modern ancient monument. The gap in the blocks for the single-track line which once lead to Hurn and Ringwood would have needed to be blocked in the event of invasion. The road and rail bridges into Christchurch were mined for demolition.

This concrete pillbox is part of Dorset Ancient Monument 832, north of the railway near the bridge over the Avon. So long as Christchurch held out as a centre of resistance, the invaders of the German VI Army from Cherbourg could not link up east–west before driving inland for Bristol. In the event they never came, owing to the RAF winning the Battle of Britain and the existence of the RN fleet. The VI Army was destroyed by Russia at Stalingrad.

Pillbox at Convent Meadows protecting the Anti-Tank Island from water-borne assault.

The airfield at Somerford was vulnerable to attack by sea or air and was defended by several different types of pillbox. This one at Mudeford Wood is of an inefficient design since it is square.

This six-sided pillbox at Somerford airfield is here being encroached upon by housing, and probably no longer exists.

These pyramid-top anti-tank obstacles at Mudeford Quay are becoming buried by the raised ground at the car park.

This pillbox at the east end of Mudeford Quay has been cut off at ground level so it shows the thickness of the walls and the stump of the central pillar anti-blast shield. Such defences can be unsightly but some survived because they were difficult to destroy. They are now recognised as part of our history and industrial archaeology.

This large pillbox at the Sandhills no longer exists, owing to the construction of sea defences. It was particularly interesting since it faced out to sea at the entrance of The Run. Usually, pillboxes were planned to give enfilade fire at beach exits. Its most novel characteristic was that it was camouflaged by a genuine beach chalet built on top.

An aerial view of the beach-chalet pillbox shows the houses Gundimore and The Anchorage in the background.

These anti-tank obstacles are at the seaward end of Avon Run Road. The pyramid tops were designed to impede tank tracks.

This heavily overgrown pillbox covers the Ringwood Road bridge over the railway at Amberwood, between Hinton and Walkford. The railway was used as a rearward defence of the coast from troops landed inland by glider or parachute. There is a particularly well-concealed pillbox built into the road bridge at Roeshott Hill which could give enfilade fire down the deep cutting; it even has an air sentry post to look out over Guss Common.

HAVING FUN

Potential volunteers for Christchurch Fire Brigade.

Royal Hampshire Regiment, now merged with Princess of Wales Royal Regiment, recruiting at Quomps –
they catch them young. The Royal Hampshire were known as the Tigers; their cap badge of tiger and rose was
nicknamed 'cat and cabbage'. Along with the Devonshire and Dorset Regiment, these units hold the Freedom
of the Borough.

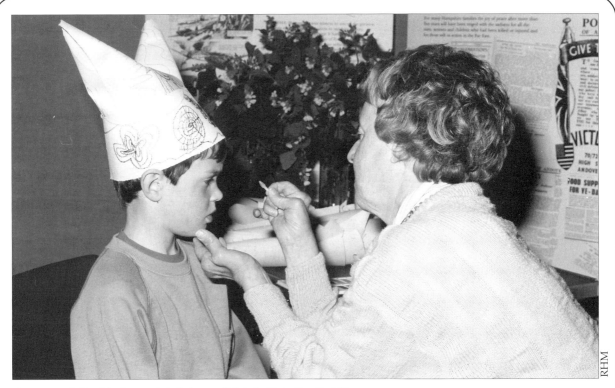

A young visitor his face painted at a craft fair held in the Red House.

A mock Court Leet held outside the Mayor's Parlour. The hayward/town crier is disputing an issue with the aletaster.

Dancers performing in the Priory Gardens during the 1978 Folk Festival. The background is a former mausoleum.

CLHS

Morris dancer makes an entrance at the Folk Festival.

CLHS

Vietnamese refugees were accommodated at Sopley and many of the families were 'adopted' by local people. Here three children are being shown around the fire-damaged Highcliffe Castle and along with their host are enjoying an ice-cream.

Vietnamese children being amused by playing at the stocks at Christchurch Castle. (These stocks were erected by the author thirty years ago and he has never remembered to ask for permission.)

Boy Scouts taking part in the Crazy Craft Race.

A close race between coxed fours at Christchurch Regatta.

Five determined-looking ladies with their racing craft outside Christchurch Rowing Club.

Miss P. Thorner names Totem *for the Christchurch Sea Rangers at Elkins Boatyard, with Canon R.P. Price attending to give the blessing, c.1956.*

Wolf Cubs on parade at Barrack Road Recreation Ground, St George's Day 1953.

Football action in Christchurch's Barrack Road Recreation Ground.

Ladies protesting at the loss of the green lung at Hoborne (pronounced Hub-bun) between Somerford and Highcliffe. Over-development remains a planning risk for the borough.

The Mayor's Eleven is batting, with the Mayor, Cllr John Morgan, displaying a certain style at the crease, Barrack Road Recreation Ground.

CLHS

This photograph of Christchurch Harbour and its entrance reveals the difficulties of navigation because of the shallows. The black line running into Christchurch Bay from Mudeford Spit is the Clarendon Rocks, the remains of a failed seventeenth-century harbour entrance.

Flying Boat over Hengistbury showing Mudeford Spit, c.1950. The aircraft may have been on trials from Poole or Calshot.

Mudeford Spit from Hengistbury Head. These huts can now sell for £70,000.

Low tide at Mudeford Spit reveals the Clarendon Rocks and some remains of the seventeenth-century attempt to create a new harbour entrance.

A concrete craft inside the harbour, once used as the head of the spit's ferry jetty.

The dramatic effects of a storm on Mudeford Spit, possibly 1953.

⚜
MUDEFORD

Mudeford Quay and The Run in about 1960. Flat-bottomed punts are in use as ferries and a salmon net is being hauled ashore in The Run. The Haven Inn lacks a café, there is no fish stall or Highcliffe Sailing Club or Lifeboat Station; an earlier café is on the site of the Sailing Club.

A view of Mudeford Quay showing the Haven in the harbour at the mouths of the Mude and the Bure.

A salmon punt in use as a ferry across The Run, the entrance to Christchurch Harbour and Mudeford. The Dutch Cottages in the photograph were built for use by dredgermen improving the navigation of the harbour as part of the River Avon Navigation Act 1664. The end of the house on the right facing The Run was the original Haven Inn, much favoured by smugglers and first mentioned in the House of Commons Journal 1699. *It was from the windows of this house that smugglers fired on a Royal Navy and Customs and Excise 'cutting-out' expedition, killing the latter's leader and winning the day at what became called the Battle of Mudeford in 1784.*

High tide and floods make Mudeford Quay an island.

Lobster pots stored at Mudeford Quay which is a registered Sea Fishery Harbour. The building is the former Haven Inn from which smugglers fired on the Navy and Revenue.

A commercial fishing boat heads back to Mudeford.

After a night hunting fish the catch has been unloaded and the decks are swabbed down.

Mudeford Haven. The ex-RN motor launch stern-on to the shore was the Mudeford Yacht Club, now the Mudeford Sailing Club which currently uses a Dutch barge at Fisherman's Bank.

113

Re-piling and raising the level of Mudeford Quay at The Run.

The new face of Mudeford Quay to The Run and tarmac car park.

The new car park was obviously much needed.

Holidaymakers returning up The Run from a 'skylark' round the bay.

Sandhills House at Mudeford, once the house of Sir George Rose MP and visited by George III, who arrived in his yacht and came ashore by means of a jetty made of bathing machines.

Gundimore, a house on the shore, east of Sandhills, designed to look like an Arab tent. It was here that Sir Walter Scott wrote much of Marmion.

Storm at Avon Beach with the Beach Café, left background, and anti-tank obstacles reused as beach erosion defences.

RHM AW

A lagoon can sometimes form off the beach at Friars Cliff and Avon, the effect of coastal drift caused by the Stour exiting at The Run. Such lagoons can trap the unwary on the sand bar when the tide comes in.

RHM

Friars Cliff and Avon beaches from the air. This photograph also shows aerials still standing at Hengistbury and was probably taken in the late 1940s before modern housing development. The black line in the sea may be anti-invasion scaffolding not yet removed.

Friars Cliff Beach looking towards Steamer Point.

Steamer Point Beach at high tide. The name derives from an abandoned steamer once used as a home on the shore, the boiler of which can be glimpsed at some low tides. The vessel had been used to tow barges of stone from France to build the second Highcliffe Castle in the 1830s.

Steamer Point is in the centre of the picture on the coast. The open space at centre right is Highcliffe Golf Course; to the left can be seen the Somerford Airfield, now long gone for redevelopment. The buildings at Steamer Point were once used by an Emergency Beach Battery, then by SRDE (the Signals Research and Development Establishment), now a Coastguard Training School. Christchurch has other golf courses at Two Riversmeet and at Iford.

⚜
STANPIT

The Rising Sun Inn at Purewell Cross, north of Stanpit. On the left of the photograph is the crossroads where Burton Road turned north to Staple Cross, and where there is now a link to Stony Lane Roundabout; to the south the road continues past the Ship in Distress Inn to Mudeford Quay and the Haven Inn. The main road continues towards Rosehott Hill, past the site of Somerford Grange, once the farm of Christchurch Priory, on to Hinton and the Cat and Fiddle Inn. At the foot of Rosehott there is a branch road to Highcliffe, past the building which was once the Isle of Wight Hoy Inn. All these pubs were once heavily involved in smuggling.

The old Stanpit Village Room, now replaced by a smart village hall.

Stanpit from the air in about 1960. The letters indicate: A – the new Ivy Cottage; B – Absolm's, once a brewery; C – the old Girl Guide Hut, resting on top of Tutton's Well, the site of a spring once used as Stanpit's only source of fresh water, strewn with stones to reduce the mud at the 'dipping place', later replaced by a bucket well where the letter C is placed, which in turn became a village pump that was closed in 1940; D – Tutton's Lodge; E – Little Stanpit. Behind Tutton's Well, where a creek comes through the red beds of Stanpit Marsh, was a quay wall and slipway used by fishermen collecting fresh water. The area was known as Stanpit Docks.

The original Guide Hut on top of Tutton's Well – wella is Anglo-Saxon for spring. The hut has now been replaced by a permanent building.

Cottages at Mudeford, c.1970.

The original Mudeford Men's Club, decked out for the Coronation in 1953. A smart permanent building now occupies the site.

The Victorian letter-box at Mudeford which is still in use.

Mother Seller's Channel at Stanpit Marsh. Hannah Seller was a widow who kept the Haven Inn during the heyday of smuggling. Her father had the Lamb Inn at Winkton. The name is spelt Siller on OS maps. The channel ran up the harbour and enabled smuggled tobacco to be carried to near the tobacco factory at Stanpit.

Crouch Hill a prehistoric barrow at Stanpit Marsh.

The River Mude enters the Haven at Christchurch Harbour at the centre of the photograph. All Saints' Church is at the right with the Avonmouth Hotel on the coast near it. The trees at centre right on the airfield are Mudeford Wood.

Fisherman's Bank from the north. The letters indicate: A – the former Coastguard HQ; B – former Coastguard cottages; C – former Watch House where the Coastguard boat was kept.

The northern end of Fisherman's Bank. The name arises from fishing boats being drawn up here for work on them and their fishing gear. There is a footpath along the land and it is registered as common, but it is privately owned and there are no common rights.

SOMERFORD AIRFIELD

This photograph, possibly by Allen White, shows Fisherman's Bank and Somerford Airfield. The camouflaged hangar facing the field at centre left was HMS Raven *a Fleet Air Arm 'stone frigate' used to equip carrier-borne aircraft with radar. The satellite aircraft factory is above the centre of the photograph. The Air Defence Experimental Establishment (1938–42), which became the Signals Research and Development Establishment, is at the top of the airfield, centre right. Bure Homage, used as the Officers' Mess of the Christchurch Advanced Landing Ground of USAAF 405 Fighter Bomber Group was just out of the picture to the right. Several pill-boxes can also be seen.*

The Airspeed, later de Havilland, aircraft factory at Somerfield Airfield. This factory made Oxford trainers, Horsa gliders and Mosquito fighter bombers during the war. Later it manufactured Venom and Sea Vixen jet fighters and the Ambassador (aka Elizabethan) airliner. The Horsa gliders were towed by obsolete bombers, used as tugs, to Tarrant Rushton, Hurn and other airfields for use by airborne landing troops. Being near the sea the airfield was vulnerable to attack. It was defended by several different types of pillbox: square, polygonal and even hydraulic, such as the Picket-Hamilton which was entered from ground level and then raised hydraulically.

Somerford Airfield in 1953, still with a grass runway. The letters indicate: A – Purewell Cross; B – The de Havilland Aircraft Factory; C – The site of Somerford Grange the home of the last prior of Christchurch after the Dissolution; E – Signals Research and Development Establishment; E – Bure Lane which leads to Humphries Bridge at the bottom right; F – Bure Homage House built by former smuggler Sophie Dawes after she had become a French baroness.

HIGHCLIFFE

RHM AW

Chewton Bunny runs inland from the centre of the picture. On the right, Nash Farm, in Hampshire, from an old-English name meaning 'at the ash tree'. The coast of Nash (again wrongly shown on maps as Naish) has eroded thanks to a lack of sea defences which have been provided at Highcliffe, on the left (west) of the Bunny. The latter word means 'a chine with a water course where reeds grow'. Since 1974 Chewton Bunny has been the boundary between Hampshire and Dorset, and the South East and South West regions.

RHM AW

Chewton Bunny where the River Chew, now called the Walkford Brook, meets the sea. Since this photograph, in 1952, the Bunny has been landscaped and the river is in a tunnel until it reaches the shore.

Once a favourite landing place for smugglers, Chewton Bunny seen before landscaping and coast defence works.

The 1832 mansion of High Cliff, was known as Highcliffe Castle before the two fires which caused so much damage around the late 1960s.

CLHS

Highcliffe Castle in a rather neglected state but before the fires so still intact. The oriel window and other carvings were brought from Les Andeleys, a French medieval château.

Highcliffe was purchased in 1977 by Christchurch Council in order to gain a beach access and car parking space. Since then over £5.24 million has been spent to restore the exterior of the buildings; much of the interior is still in a damaged condition and is not open to the public but its woodland and garden are. Here it is seen in 1975 after damage from fires.

The roofless Highcliffe Castle, surrounded by bungalows on two sides.

RHM

Brook House, Mudeford, demolished in 1967.

RHM

Bure Homage Lodge, Bure Lane, c.1970.

CLHS

Bure Homage, demolished for redevelopment in the 1970s.

RHM

Hoborne House, demolished for redevelopment, was once the home of General Brown who was Chief Air Raid Warden for Christchurch during the war.

CLHS

The west face of Hoborne House, one of so many noble buildings lost to redevelopment.

Beacon Lodge which belonged to Highcliffe Castle.

Saulflands the dower house of Hoborne House. Built in 1908 it is now converted into flats but without the vegetation growing over it. During the war it was the billet of ATS cooks, clerks, telephonists and other staff at the Steamer Point Coast Defence Battery.

This was Cliff House, which became the Gallion pub in the 1970s and is now the Hinton Oak Inn.

Clare Court which stood opposite the Globe Inn until redeveloped in the 1960s.

Wingfield House. Only the name Wingfield survived, as a Ward name, and now that too is gone.

Nea House, a name derived from n'eam meaning 'at the water'; demolished in 1939, but survives as a road name, and as Nea Meadows.

Latimers – this survives.

Holmhurst Lodge, before tarmac road and a pavement.

Chewton Mill House in an old photograph, another building that has survived.

Highcliffe village centre, probably an Allen White photograph, c.1950.

ARCHAEOLOGY

Bronze Age Barrow at Wick, showing some damage by the roots of trees, typical of the many surviving barrows in the area.

The Mill Steam end of the burgh wall, marked by a very large ironstone. The wall was of earth and turf faced with stone and topped by a fighting platform and a palisade. The Mill Steam was the eastern defence backed by a palisade.

Stone tumble from the Anglo-Saxon burgh wall of the ninth century, designed to keep Viking raiders out of the town. The photograph looks east down a slight slope to the Mill Stream in 1971.

CLHS

The effort was rewarded by finding the ironstone tumble from the face of the wall which, according to the **Burghal Hidage** of AD911, would have required 470 warriors to defend it. The wall ran only to Whitehall since beyond the River Stour came to that point. A large ironstone at the corner of a cottage in Silver Street at Whitehall is probably a similar stone to the one found near the Mill Steam end of the wall.

CLHS AW

Excavations behind the houses on the east side of Millhams Street lead down to the Mill Stream and proved that a wattle palisade existed.

The Dolphin Inn was demolished for redevelopment and excavation took place in 1974–75. It was a site with wells and latrines, building remains and artefacts including medieval arrowheads.

The southeast corner of the Dolphin site.

A medieval well.

A more modern well next to a cesspit?

The base of a medieval wall with flagstone entrance.

Archaeologist at work ... with site marked out by a grid.

Ditches or holes cut into the natural strata can be revealing but not when out of reach under other buildings.

Excavations at the south side of what became Saxon Square, 1976.

The ring ditch of one of two Bronze Age barrows found west of the Mill Stream in 1977–78 under what is now the Pioneer Store car park. Pagan Saxons had focused their cemetery around these two barrows. Finding these graves confirmed that the Anglo-Saxon Chronicle was accurate in its claims to early arrival in Wessex.

Excavation on south side of Mayor's Parlour in 1981.

The acid soil of Christchurch erodes skeletons but leaves magnesium traces visible in the gravel. The skull is partly preserved due to impregnation by iron although at first it caused excitement as it was mistaken for the remains of helmet. The spear heads, shield bosses, knives and brooches survived better than the bones.

In 1981 a small excavation to the south of the pagan Saxon cemetery sought to discover its size. It appears not to have spread south towards the burgh, although it may spread west towards Bargates or north to Beaconsfield.

⚜
BURTON

RHM

A thatched cottage at Burton possibly once lived in by Southey the poet. Burton takes its name from the ton – enclosure – belonging to the burgh – fort.

CLHS H.G. Miles-Berry

The old Game Larder at Burton, demolished for redevelopment.

Staple Cross, where Burton Road becomes Salisbury Road at the junction with Ambury Lane, near Hawthorn Lane. The Cross is shown here before 1944 when the top was broken by an American tank. It is also before the bypass raised the ground level around the Cross so that it no longer stands on a mound. The staple referred to what was probably the export tax on wool, which may have been weighed here for export outside the Priory Manor, so avoiding a further tax to the Church.

Dairy House Farm, Burton, undergoing rethatching.

Burton Green.

The village of Burton from the air, c.1980.

St Michael's Church, Sopley, north of Burton. This medieval church has both a female and a male sheela-na-gig (an obscene carving meant to drive away the Devil) on its north-transept exterior, with a 'tongue-puller' – another form of insulting carving – inside the church. It is on a mound and may have been a pagan site like Christchurch Minster before the Priory.

Sopley Mill on the Avon in Hampshire.

Sopley church and Mill from the air.

Winkton hamlet and River Avon, c.1960.

TRANSPORT

Water-borne traffic was the original cause for the location of Christchurch but the shallow harbour now restricts the size of craft.

The Lymington Road at Chewton. The first-ever reinforced concrete bridge.

A horse dray of Hayball & Sons in the 1950s.

153

Trolleybus in Church Street outside the Dolphin. The inn site is now redeveloped but the bus turntable remains.

A BAC One-Eleven airliner at Hurn Air Show 1978. Until 1974 Hurn parish was part of the Ringwood Rural District. The parish has less than 200 electors but covers a wide area including all of Bournemouth International Airport and its associated industries. Hurn parish also accommodates the Alice in Wonderland Family Park and a Ski Centre.

The 'Ringwood Flyer' from Brockenhurst at Holmsley Railway Station, now tea rooms. This station was the original Christchurch Road railway station in 1847. It was then a 7-mile walk to Christchurch.

The old railway line on Town Common, from Christchurch to Hurn and Ringwood, opened in 1862. On the left is St Catherine's Hill on the right is the Keeper's Cottage at Cowherds Marsh (now called Cowards Marsh).

CLHS AW

A train leaving Hurn railway station, which closed to passengers in 1935 and for freight in 1938.

RHM K. B. Hastie

Hurn railway station in 1977 before it was reopened as a pub, the Avon Causeway.

The Bournemouth to Birkenhead Express leaving Christchurch in 1954. Concrete anti-tank 5ft cubes can be seen on the right of the photograph. These are now scheduled as Dorset Ancient Monument 832. They made Christchurch a promontory fort as in Saxon times.

The Royal Wessex drawn by a diesel-electric engine entering Christchurch Station in 1953. The line to London via Brockenhurst from Christchurch opened in 1888.

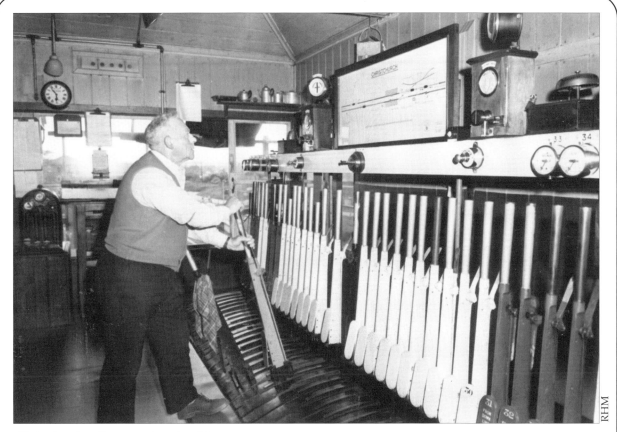

Christchurch railway station signal box.

A Battle-of-Britain-class engine drawing an express from Waterloo via Christchurch, over the Stour on the run to Bournemouth, Poole and Weymouth.

A West-Country-class engine, Taunton, *entering Christchurch Station in 1966. Note the height of the signal box to give a clear view of the track.*

A West-Country-class engine, Okehampton, *at Christchurch for Southbourne on Sea on the run to London Waterloo.*